I CAN DO ALL THINGS THROUGH CHRIST WHO STRENGTHENS ME

Philippians 4:13

Tammy Mills

To God for giving me the wisdom to create my first children's book.
To Solana my first adorable granddaughter.
To the beautiful children of Saint Jude.

My beautiful ones, don't forget to review and reflect for growth. Remember, I encourage readers to always reference back to this book to add pictures, read the affirmations/scriptures, and answer the questions as they become themselves.

You were born with a purpose, and you hold the keys to your own destiny.

1.)What is your full name?_____

2.)What are your parents' names?_____

3.)What is/are your sibling(s) name(s)?_____

4.)Do you have a favorite pet? _____

5.)What is your favorite color?_____

6.)What makes you happy?_____

7.)What is your favorite subject in school?_____

8.)What is your least favorite subject in school?_____

9.)What makes you sad?_____

10.)Who do you want to become?_____

Selfie

Selfies

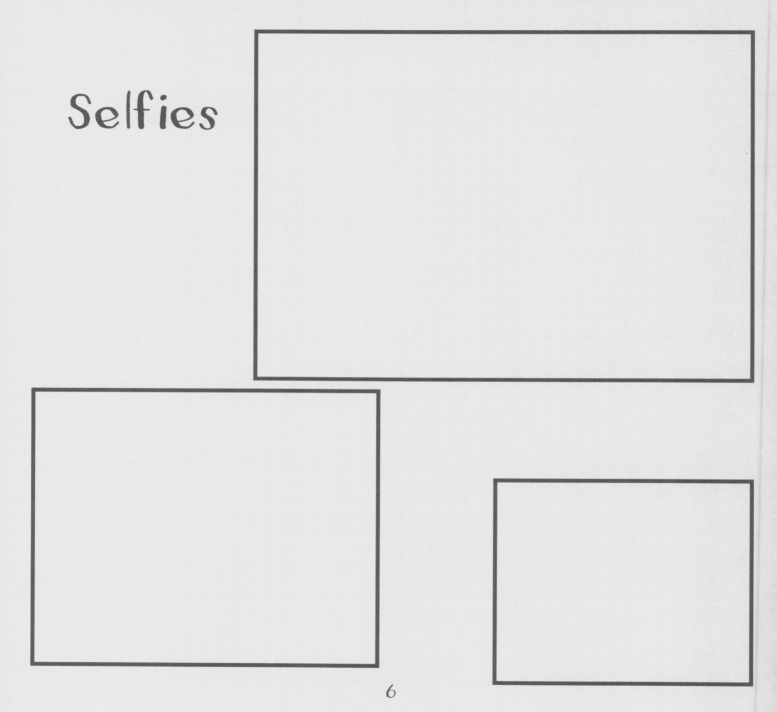

6

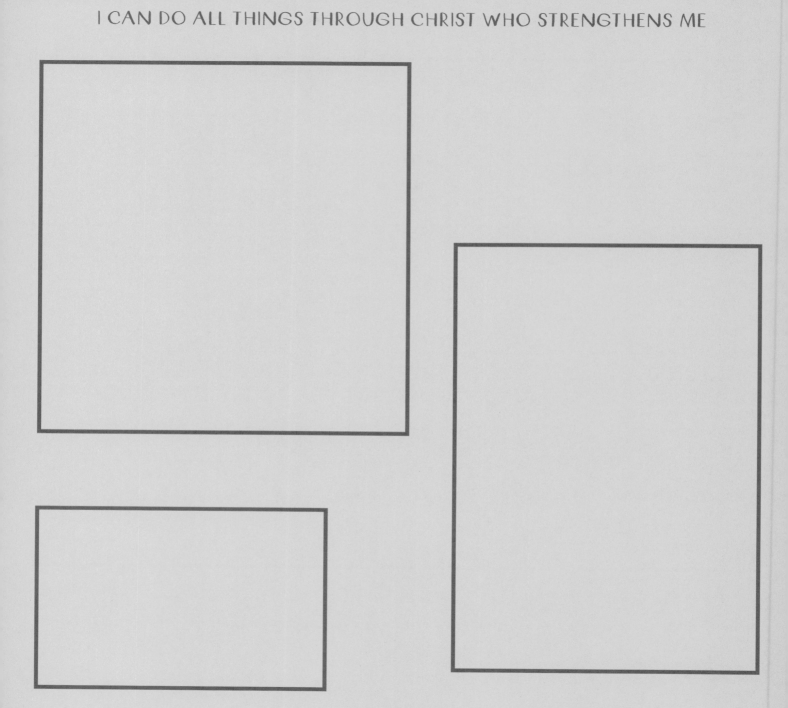

I CAN LOVE LIKE— GOD

Name all the people you LOVE.

_____

_____

_____

_____

_____

_____

_____

_____

_____

"For God so loved the word that he gave his only begotten son, that whosoever believe on him will have everlasting life."
John 3:16

In the following pages, write down your thoughts about being LOVED.

_____

_____

_____

_____

_____

_____

_____

_____

_____

_____

_____

_____

_____

_____

_____

_____

_____

_____

_____

_____

_____

_____

_____

_____

_____

I CAN HAVE FAITH LIKE—ABRAHAM

Who said without FAITH it's impossible to please me?

_____

_____

_____

_____

_____

_____

_____

_____

_____

"By faith Abraham, when he was tried, offered up Isaac: and he that had received the promises offered up his only begotten son."
Hebrews 11:17 (KJV)

In the following pages, write down your thoughts about FAITH.

_____

_____

_____

_____

_____

_____

_____

_____

_____

_____

_____

_____

_____

_____

_____

_____

_____

_____

_____

_____

_____

_____

_____

_____

_____

_____

_____

_____

_____

_____

_____

_____

_____

_____

_____

_____

_____

_____

I CAN PRAY LIKE— JESUS

Who do you PRAY for?

_____

_____

_____

_____

_____

_____

_____

_____

_____

"And it came to pass, that, as he was praying
in a certain place, when he ceased, one of his
disciples said unto him, Lord, teach us to pray,
as John also taught his disciples."
Luke 11:1

In the following pages, write down your thoughts about PRAYER.

_____

_____

_____

_____

_____

_____

_____

_____

_____

_____

_____

_____

I CAN DO ALL THINGS THROUGH CHRIST WHO STRENGTHENS ME

I CAN DO ALL THINGS THROUGH CHRIST WHO STRENGTHENS ME

I CAN BELIEVE LIKE— MARY

What are you BELIEVING for?

_____

_____

_____

_____

_____

_____

_____

_____

_____

_____

"And Mary said, 'Behold the handmaid of the Lord; be it unto me according to thy word.' And the angel departed from her."
Luke 1:38

In the following pages, write down your thoughts about BELIEVING.

_____

_____

_____

_____

_____

_____

_____

_____

_____

_____

_____

_____

_____

_____

_____

_____

_____

_____

_____

_____

_____

_____

_____

_____

_____

_____

_____

_____

_____

_____

_____

_____

_____

_____

_____

_____

_____

_____

_____

_____

_____

_____

_____

_____

_____

_____

_____

_____

_____

_____

_____

I AM SPECIAL LIKE— ELISHA

Why are you SPECIAL?

_____
_____
_____
_____
_____
_____
_____
_____
_____

"And it came to pass, when they were gone over, that Elijah said unto Elisha, Ask what I shall do for thee, before I be taken away from thee. And Elisha said , I pray thee, let a double portion of thy spirit be upon me"
2 Kings 2:9

In the following pages, write down your thoughts about being SPECIAL.

_____

_____

_____

_____

_____

_____

_____

_____

_____

_____

_____

_____

I CAN SMILE LIKE—JOB

What makes you SMILE?

_____

_____

_____

_____

_____

_____

_____

_____

_____

_____

_____

_____

_____

_____

_____

_____

_____

_____

"If I say, I will forget my complaint, I will change my expression, and smile."
Job 9:27 (NIV)

In the following pages, write down your thoughts about SMILING.

_____

_____

_____

_____

_____

_____

_____

_____

_____

_____

_____

_____

_____

_____

_____

_____

_____

_____

_____

_____

_____

_____

_____

_____

_____

_____

_____

_____

_____

_____

_____

_____

_____

_____

_____

_____

_____

_____

I AM CONFIDENT LIKE—DEBORAH

Give an example of how you've been CONFIDENT.

_____

_____

_____

_____

_____

_____

_____

_____

_____

"And she dwelt under the palm tree of Deborah between Ramah and Bethel in mount Ephraim; and the children of Israel came up to her for judgement."
Judges 4:5

In the following pages, write down your thoughts about being CONFIDENT.

_____

_____

_____

_____

_____

_____

_____

_____

_____

_____

_____

_____

_____

_____

_____

_____

_____

_____

_____

_____

_____

_____

_____

_____

_____

_____

_____

I AM STRONG LIKE— SAMSON

Name a friend who's STRONG.

_____

_____

_____

_____

_____

_____

_____

_____

_____

_____

"And the Spirit of the Lord came mightily upon him, and he rent him as he would have rent a kid, and he had nothing in his hand."
Judges 14:6

In the following pages, write down your thoughts about being STRONG.

_____

_____

_____

_____

_____

_____

_____

_____

_____

_____

_____

_____

I CAN DANCE LIKE— DAVID

How do you feel when you DANCE?

_____

_____

_____

_____

_____

_____

_____

_____

_____

_____

"And David danced before the Lord with
all his might .And David was wearing a linen
ephod."
2 Samuel 6:14

In the following pages, write down your thoughts about DANCING.

_____

_____

_____

_____

_____

_____

_____

_____

_____

_____

_____

I AM VICTORIOUS LIKE— JEHOSHAPHAT

Name a few VICTORIES you have had.

_____

_____

_____

_____

_____

_____

_____

_____

"Ye shall not need to fight in this battle: set yourselves, stand ye still, and see the salvation of the Lord with you, O Judah and Jerusalem: fear not, nor be dismayed; tomorrow go out against them: for the Lord will be with you."
2 Chronicles 20:17

In the following pages, write down your thoughts about being VICTORIUS.

_____

_____

_____

_____

_____

_____

_____

_____

_____

_____

_____

_____

_____

_____

_____

_____

_____

_____

_____

_____

_____

_____

_____

_____

_____

I AM CHOSEN LIKE— ISRAEL

What makes you UNIQUE?

_____

_____

_____

_____

_____

_____

_____

_____

_____

_____

"But I have chosen Jerusalem, that my name might be there; and have chosen David to be over my people Israel."
2 Chronicles 6:6

In the following pages, write down your thoughts about being CHOSEN.

_____

_____

_____

_____

_____

_____

_____

_____

_____

_____

_____

_____

_____

_____

_____

_____

_____

_____

_____

_____

_____

_____

_____

_____

_____

_____

_____

_____

_____

_____

_____

_____

_____

_____

_____

_____

_____

_____

I AM LOYAL LIKE— RUTH

What makes you LOYAL?

_____
_____
_____
_____
_____
_____
_____
_____
_____

"But Ruth said, Do not urge me to leave you or return from following you. For where you go I will go, and where you lodge I will lodge. Your people shall be my people, and your God my God"
Ruth 1:16

In the following pages, write down your thoughts about being LOYAL.

_____
_____
_____
_____
_____
_____
_____
_____
_____
_____
_____
_____

_____

_____

_____

_____

_____

_____

_____

_____

_____

_____

_____

_____

_____

_____

_____

_____

_____

_____

_____

_____

_____

_____

_____

_____

_____

_____

_____

I AM PROTECTED LIKE—DANIEL

How do you feel PROTECTED?

_____
_____
_____
_____
_____
_____
_____
_____
_____
_____

"May God has sent his angel, and hath shut
the lions' mouths,that they have not hurt me:
forasmuch as before him innocence was
found in me:and also before thee. O king,
have I done no hurt."
Daniel 6:22

In the following pages, write down your thoughts about being PROTECTED.

_____

_____

_____

_____

_____

_____

_____

_____

_____

_____

_____

_____

I CAN BE BRAVE LIKE— MOSES

What have you done to be BRAVE?

_____
_____
_____
_____
_____
_____
_____
_____
_____
_____
_____
_____
_____
_____
_____

"Then Moses stretched out his hand over the sea; and the Lord caused the sea to go back by a strong east wind all that night, and made the sea into dry land, and the waters divided."
Exodus 14:21 (KJV)

In the following pages, write down your thoughts about being BRAVE.

_____

_____

_____

_____

_____

_____

_____

_____

_____

_____

_____

_____

I CAN FIGHT LIKE— JOSHUA

Name your favorite HERO?

_____

_____

_____

_____

_____

_____

_____

_____

_____

_____

"And Joshua did unto them as the Lord bade him: he houghed their horses, and burnt their chariots with fire."
Joshua 11:9

In the following pages, write down your thoughts about being a HERO.

_____

_____

_____

_____

_____

_____

_____

_____

_____

_____

_____

_____

_____

I AM COURAGEOUS LIKE—ESTHER

How have you shown COURAGE?

_____

_____

_____

_____

_____

_____

"Go, gather together all the Jews that are present in Shushan, and fast ye for me, and neither eat nor drink three days, night or day: I also and my maidens will fast likewise; and so will I go in unto the king, which is not according to the law:and if I perish, I perish."
Esther 4:16

In the following pages, write down your thoughts about being COURAGEOUS.

_____

_____

_____

_____

_____

_____

_____

_____

_____

_____

_____

_____

_____

_____

_____

_____

_____

_____

_____

_____

_____

_____

_____

_____

Believe in yourself and never give up on your dreams.

Add a picture of your heart's desire.

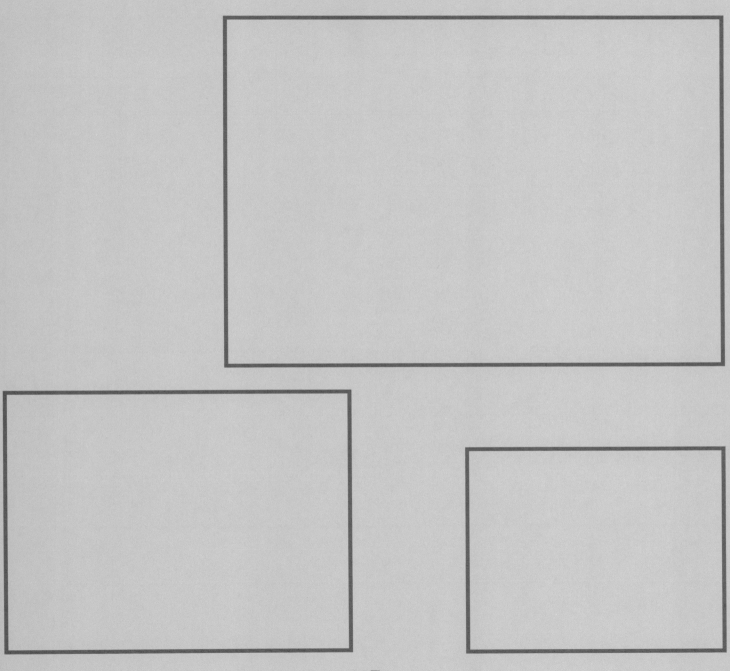

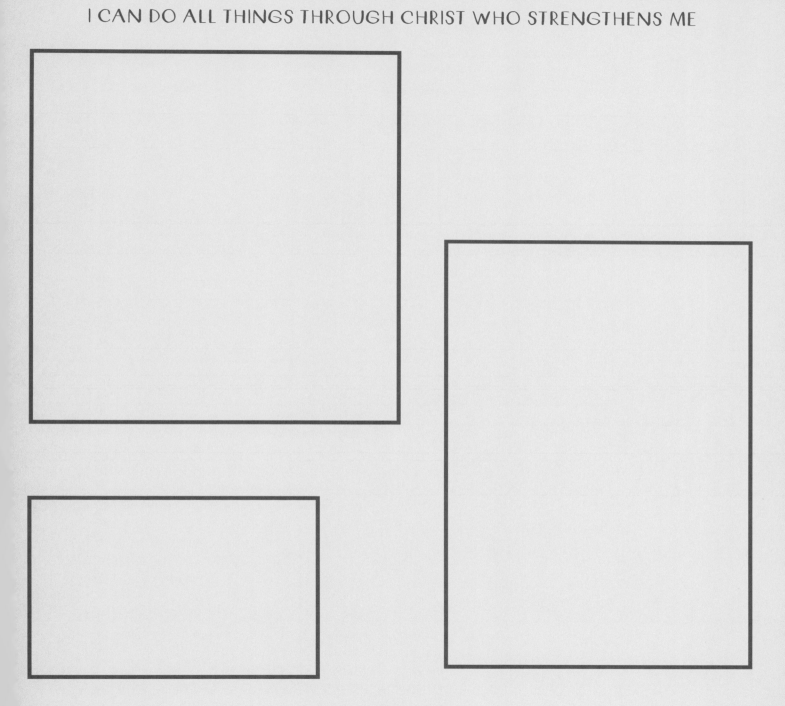

My name is Tammy Mills. I am a Christian, and I am married to my handsome husband Roneil. We have been married for 30 years and we have 2 beautiful daughters, Paris and Tamia. We also have an adorable granddaughter named Solana. I graduated from St.Paul's College with an BS in Criminal Justice and a Associate Degree in Human Service Technology. I am a recording artist, author, publisher, motivational speaker, entrepreneur and fitness/life coach. I enjoy spending time with my family, working out, reading, shopping and traveling.

I CAN DO ALL THINGS THROUGH CHRIST WHO STRENGTHENS ME

Philippians 4:13